Our Global Community

Clothing

Lisa Easterling

Heinemann
LIBRARY

www.heinemann.co.uk/library

Visit our website to find out more information about Heinemann Library books.

To order:

 Phone 44 (0) 1865 888066

Send a fax to 44 (0) 1865 314091

 Visit the Heinemann Bookshop at www.heinemann.co.uk/library to browse our
 catalogue and order online.

First published in Great Britain by Heinemann Library, Halley Court, Jordan Hill, Oxford OX2 8EJ, part of Harcourt Education. Heinemann is a registered trademark of Harcourt Education Ltd.

Editorial: Diyan Leake and Cassie Mayer
Design: Joanna Hinton-Malivoire
Picture research: Ruth Smith
Production: Duncan Gilbert

Origination: Chroma Graphics (Overseas) Pte Ltd
Printed and bound in China by South China
 Printing Company Ltd

ISBN 978 0 431 19108 9
11 10 09 08 07
10 9 8 7 6 5 4 3 2 1

British Library Cataloguing in Publication Data

Easterling, Lisa
  Clothing. - (Our global community)
  1. Clothing and dress - Juvenile literature 2. Costume - Juvenile literature
  I. Title
  391

Acknowledgements

The publishers would like to thank the following for permission to reproduce photographs: Alamy pp. **9** (Blend Images), **15** (Around the World in a Viewfinder), **23** (Blend Images); Corbis pp. **4** (James Leynse), **5** (Michael Reynolds/epa), **6** (Galen Rowell), **8** (Fabio Cardoso/zefa), **10**, **11**, **12** (Jose Luis Pelaez, Inc.), **13** (Yang Liu), **16** (Penny Tweedie), **17** (Daniel Lainé), **18** (Peter Turnley), **19** (Roger Ressmeyer), **20** (Sergio Pitamitz), **23** (Yang Liu; Michael Reynolds/epa); Getty Images pp. **7** (Image Bank), **14** (Robert Harding).

Contents

Clothing

People wear clothes.

Clothes protect your body.

Types of clothes

Clothes protect you from the cold.

Clothes protect you from the sun.

Some clothes are for work.

Some work clothes are uniforms.

Some clothes are for indoor sports.

Some clothes are for outdoor hobbies.

These clothes are for people who have finished college.

These clothes are for a bride.

Clothing around the world

In Japan some people wear kimonos.

A kimono has a wide belt.

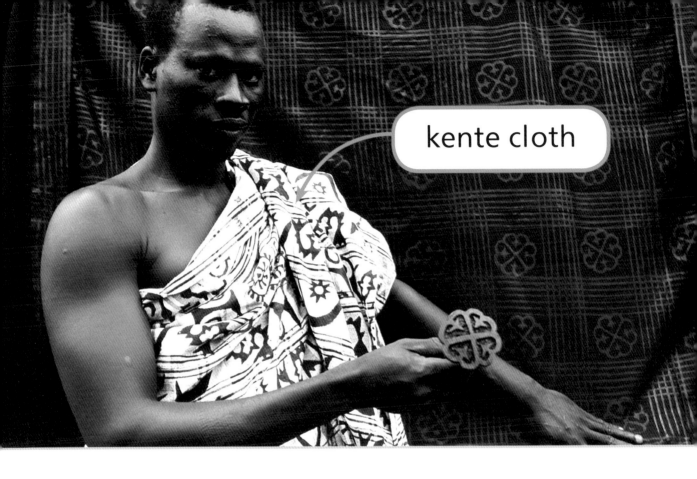

kente cloth

In Africa some people wear a kente.

A kente is worn on special days.

In India some women wear saris.

sarong

In Bali some men wear sarongs.

All around the world, people wear different clothes.

What kind of clothes do you wear?

What are clothes made of?

- Clothes are made of cotton. Cotton comes from a plant.

- Clothes are made of linen. Linen comes from a plant.

- Clothes are made of wool. Wool comes from sheep.

- Clothes are made of silk. Silk comes from silkworms.

Picture glossary

 **bride** a woman on the day she gets married

 **protect** keep from harm

 **uniform** clothing that tells where you work

Index

Notes for parents and teachers

Before reading

Ask the children why they wear clothes. Do they wear different clothes at different times of the year? Why do the clothes change? What do they like wearing best? Can they think of an occasion when they wore special clothes? Talk about the different occasions when they might wear special clothes – for games, at a party, or sleeping.

After reading

Talking about clothes. Let the children work in pairs and go and choose some dressing-up clothes that they want to wear. Encourage them to talk about the clothes they have chosen. What did they like about the clothes? Talk about colours, uniforms, and characters.

A clothing race. Divide the children into teams. Put a selection of clothes in a line a running distance in front of each team. The first child runs to the first item and puts it on. The next member of the team then runs to the next item and puts it on, and so on. The winning team is the one that first puts on all the clothes.

Weaving. Make a weaving base by cutting six even lines across a piece of card, ensuring that the strips stay intact on the base. Give each child different coloured strips of card and show them how to weave these in and out of the base, first by going over and under and next by going under then over. Display their weaving on the classroom wall.